Poetry
In
Slow-motion

Special dedication to my Aunt Brenda Ennis who passed away January 3, 2020 may you Rest in Peace. I love you.

Dedications

Rasheeda was raised in a household full of talented women. A little fun fact, her oldest aunt on her mother's side Mary Chambers used to wake young Rasheeda up out of her sleep to perform Diana Ross for her friends. Joyce Chambers Rasheeda's youngest aunt was an amazing singer. Aunt Brenda, Uncle James and Uncle Lou also could sing. Rasheeda's mother Virginia Chambers is the one that she has the passion for art.

Freddy Wiltshire Rasheeda's father is where she gets the passion for rhyming. Rasheeda grew up surrounded by a lot of love. Her grandmother Mozella Chambers Showed all her children how to Value one another. This book is dedicated to my family, Some have now gone to heaven. My mother, my father, my grandmother, all three of my aunts and both of my uncles. Thank God for Aunt Josette, Aunt Sue and all my cousins. Please show those that you hold dear to you how much you appreciate them. I want to show the world that is possible to live out your wonderful dreams positively. Keep dreaming big. Positive poetry! Peace and possibilities!

Coolgmack for once again for making my dream come true. Amazing success is in both of our future. keep on writing. God bless

Foreword

Rasheeda Wiltshire known as SlowMotion to poetry world, is glad to present a collection of poetry. Play with my words, read in between the lines. SlowMotion loves metaphors and alliterations. In this book the rhyme scheme is different and fun.

This unique collection of poetry a walk in the world of SlowMotion. Relatable situations. Loving words. Takes you to a place of a hurting heart, overcoming pain. Bravery and bold to rebuild. Poems about Mending Hearts. Coming together and finding understanding.

I'm excited for the world to read my words.

I want to show the world that is possible to live out your wonderful dreams positively. Keep dreaming Big. **Positive poetry! Peace and possibilities!**

Acknowledgements

To Virginia Chambers and Frederick Wiltshire my parents

Coolgmack's BookKing
            Publishing
                    Yonkers, NY
                    coolgmack@gmail.com
                            coolgmack.com

0

The Writer

I sit here in sex

Soaking in ambition

I stopped to listen

The heart starts beating faster

Then the pulsating rhythm

of my position

Stooping to her level

I'll leave

to come

and we are as one

She follows me and that orgasmic way

Pounding the power

she already knows where I'm coming from...

Her words excite me

Her rhyme invites me

To a world I've never been

And we do it all again

Talking about our dreams

Understanding what all this means

And we are engaging in an intellectual intercourse

Her climax blows out my brain cells

I reek of her smells

This is no ordinary engagement

My tolerance is patient

I fuck her and make love to her at the same time

As her words in the background are on rewind

Potent poetry arouses me

Stains

Words damage

Unable to manage

Stopped in tracks

Of matter of past facts

Hits in the face

With that volume

That Bass

Tones of voices

Left without any choices

Left lonely

No, one will ever think that they own me

Fought for my freedom

Cried over my wisdom

Learning the truth

was my proof

I left that mark

that bite was definitely

Bigger than that bark

Now standing stronger

Back then I could not take it any longer

Your weapon was talking

My weapon became walking

The pain stains

Artistic Collaboration

letter to letter

Line for line

word to mine

Back and forth in and out

Breaking down the love for this explaining what it's all about

A poetic collaboration

Artistic formation

Birthing beautiful vocabulary

Watch it blossoming

Option for option

Our choice

Our voice Journey to that place

Watch it all become what it is meant to be

So beautifully

Written

Clearly

Focus vision

Walk with me

To the possibility

Our purpose

it is worth all of this

Word Bliss word bliss

Bae

Before

anyone

else

You can find my Bae sipping a latte in a poetry cafe.

you can find my Bae at the beach on any giving day

soaking up that sun ray!

Gorgeous as always if I may say.

You can find my Bae reciting my poetry.

For My Bae is my biggest fan...

For I, My Bae is the one who understands...

And I "get" My Bae in every way...

You can find My Bae driving all people crazy...

You can find My Bae being that natural source.

Watch as our love Takes its course!

Because my Bae is not a battle, but our passion is brutal.

Fireworks and shooting stars! Violins and guitars

You can hear love music playing in the background,

Stop and listen for that sound.

It's my bae that I've found!

You can find My Bae

being my true romantic story!

It's My Bae who makes me extremely happy!

And I do everything to Satisfy My Bae in every way!

You can find My Bae representing we!

And where you find Bae you find me!

Because it's us that's entwine, you see!

Drugs

Drugs on the mugs of the unspoken

they're all choking

smoke in folks faces

exclusive places

Dark and dingy, stalked and stingy

On the prowl that Wild Child

In search for that mental Escape

That addiction is not up for debate

Flowing through the blood streams

crashing dreams

Seeping down in the sewers

And these are the suitors

Clever and caught

by that little thing they brought

Non-Stop

feeling as if they're on top

Until it all comes Crashing Down

And real rough reality is found

Back on the stroll paying that toll

Because Dem streets are wicked

And that addiction is just too hard for them to kick it

Deja vu's

not daring to try to live in their shoes

Because that rough road is paved with broken
glass and traps

Chasing That High running dem lapse

Day in and day out

this is what that life is all about

Nodding their aspirations are rotting

This is what gives them that drive

No longer feeling alive

Looking for helping hands

someone to relate

someone that understands

But then again

Afraid for it to All end

Poison

That powerful

potent potion,

pulling and pulsating

through and at my brain

Making it hard for me to

Focus on what's truly

important

Sip by sip I would drift

13

Mad at past problems

I posed poorly pouting

Standing for hours, feeling

Tears showers

Soaking Awoken unclear

Statements

Wondering if I had made

any other arrangements

Staggering,

Grabbing for

arguments

That are not mine to defend

Praying for this pain to end

Falling deeper than I ever did

Bleeding and battered,

I place my bid

My metamorphosis

wondering if it was going to

get worse than this

Unrecognizable, staring

at my image in the mirror

it all became clearer

Polluting my precious pureness

No one could ignore this

I was sinking all because of my drinking

Assaults, it all had to come to a halt

It would take some time

to repair my mind

From all that damage I've done to it

So difficult to pull myself out of

That dark pit

I am free from captivity

Now I see brighter possibilities

TRIALS AND TRIBULATIONS

We have been sucked dry

until we have no more tears to cry

Pleasure became pain

This is how we maintain

Love's a hassle

We sit on the Beach building a sandcastle

Princess to princess

Searching for happiness

18

Pink flowers and blue dresses

As the ocean expresses

Past Loves we had lost

As life takes its course

Daring to jump in the sea

washing away our history of crazy

The waves seem not to phrase we

We surf

for all it's worth

19

The trials and tribulations

The roads, paths and stations

We walk

we swim

we ride

we fly

We have been sucked dry

Until we have no more tears to cry

But her and I know why

Deeper meanings in between the lines

Reading all the signs

No longer oppressed

As her and I stopped to rest

We were Beach bound

We took that look around

Soaked up the sun rays and lost some pounds

New lights and ocean sounds

We sat on the horizon

Sky gliding

Comprehended the surface

Never again to feel worthless

Mother Earth planet these important seeds

Received what we wanted and understood our needs

Now we know what it all means

Turning two princesses into Queens

Dreams are now reality

Teaching others of our morality

Knew New !!!

We write our wrongs

I want to lay in your arms

Wanting to hold the pain away

Counting the minutes until the day

We become partners on this path

A very important quality you have

You make me laugh

Knowing how hard it is out here

Watching you conquer your fear

I do the same

Seeing myself in your eyes

Understanding the whys

Fly

My peace of mind mine
Oh, how fine
Fine.......
You are, regular by far
You are uniquely sexy mixed up crazy
When I'm around you the whole world is hazy
I only have eyes for you
And when you do what you do
I want to be stuck to you like glue
You got that Bang Bang
Cause you know you that thang thang
You're not afraid to show it off
But when other people start to stare at you,
I start to morph
I go into jealous mode
And then my feelings unfold
Everyone can see how much you mean to me
And I'm showing it off
like it's my metal cuz, you bring out my Revel
Can you match my work?
you get on my level
I love how you challenge my authority
I stare at you and think all is not worthy
You fly fly
You that high high
I can't come down
From

And when you call me I always come

24

memories

Big

Sweet

Letters about us

Hold my hand again

Not afraid to fall in my arms We

felt safe together

Tear stains on my shoulder

Yours tattooed on me

And I don't mind

Secrets searching for a home

You found me

Standing in front of many

25

who couldn't see the truth?

Touch my heart again

Smile at me

Make all the rhymes comprehensive

It seemed as if no one else understood

Broken however fighting to find all of the missing pieces

Taking back by your beautiful

As we both know that it goes deeper than the skin

Your eyes would keep me in place

As if the world only revolves around us

Hug me again

I want to hold you forever if you let me

Growth

Awareness

I hope you hear this

Observe the words

Absorb the love

Doing all of the above

Live

Love

Learn

Laugh

Step hard to make your own path

The overwhelming thing

that brings Us to a place of Solitude

Commonly

Recognizing the mood

The shift

Writing out messages that are only meant to uplift

The soil is fertile for the growth

Do both

Be placed then planted

You are placed in the soil

So, you can grow

plant other seeds from the knowledge you know

Soaking up sessions

Education

Lessons

Teaching others

to appreciate life's blessings

Quality Inn questions

Exploring what may seem impossible

Enjoy the obstacle

Be amazed at the accomplishments

Realize the sequence

The patterns positively progressing

So what is the lesson

To live

To love

To learn

To laugh

To teach positivity

That is growth

It's poetry

It is Oral fixation poetry

concentrating on the word stimulation

The Conversation

It is linguistic masturbation

However, it is not just self-gratification

Poetry the comprehension of the rearranging

The format and Concepts

pro-ject the project

The vocabulary becomes the object

Focus on the subjects

Poetry remains the topic

Erupting

so, touching

very much relevant

no destruction

it's all about building up

positively

Express freely

Properly placing poetry

Where its meant to be

Fast then slowly

Lyrical Orgasms

for those word spasms

Artistically written on the atmosphere

Amazingly done without fear

Its poetry Baby

I'll be good to you

I want to ride with you

fly with you

get sexually high with you

grow with you

everywhere I'll go with you

tell you

smell you

of course, I want to feel you

I want to know the real you

see you been on my mind

like constantly

but it doesn't bother me

because you're like an ease through the stress

and I must confess

I've been daydreaming about you

wondering if I could spend some time alone with you

give me your number and I can talk on the phone with you.

Every time you're around my heart starts
beating faster and faster

Believe me it's not sex that I'm after

I want to know you

I will be good to you

just let me show you

what I could do to you

33

Platform

I see myself on this platform

As I perform.

I say words not songs.

They are bobbing their heads to the melody.

Can you follow me?

Sounds good to the ears

as words appear

to move them in a way of understanding.

not demanding

as I am able to hold everyone's attention.

on all dimensions.

every word they heard.

eyes open and so are their hearts.

awareness I Spark.

I cry out with all I have

and all I had.

honoring my mom and my dad.

by standing up for what I believe in.

never bow never been.

A hand or two I will lend.

Remember they are my own to loan.

Speaking teaching as I have been taught.

They understand the fight and why I have fought.

I see myself on this platform and I perform.

Words that are warm

there is no wondering why I am here

my words explain it all.

It has been instilled so I shell install.

The knowledge, the freedom and the growth

this is my oath.

I see myself on this platform and I perform.

Wordplay

Play with my words

I urge you to

merging to

Tantalizing vocabulary

Stimulating the very

Conversation

Feeling the flirtation

From A to Z

Expanding your vocabulary

Just for me

Playfully

Bracing me

Words are chasing me

I love the entwine

adoring the interaction

The amazing words are the attraction

Your words I make all mine

Pleasing my mental

From difficult to simple

Dictionary to thesaurus

And I'm craving for more of this

Caught up torn up

As words erupted

Ignite Me excite me

With your ability

Express your vocabulary

Bonding on that passion

Young but old fashioned

Words that are crashing

The elements the very suspense

What will come next

The context

Visualizing each letter

As you keep it smart and Beyond clever

New Addiction

(CoolGmack)
If this isn't love
then why do I feel this way?
Every day it's a new addition
she's the new edition that I crave
when she talks...
I listen to what she has to say
she's my new addiction
Her walk is vicious....
Her attention I pay

(Slowmotion)
So here I lay
Dreams unfulfilled
Plans we will build
There's so many questions
Why I feel this way?
Her heart's love
I will never go astray
nor will I second guess it
She's just that new edition
Add her to my heart and soul
like addition she makes me whole
I'm hoping and wishing
I made plans

and she understands me
Why must it be this way
to her.... all of my attention I pay
on my mind she always just stays
not only on Sundays
but on every other day
she gives me new visions
that I cannot display

(CoolGmack)
With her permission I stayed
She's my sunshine after tremendous rain
I rather live in a cave than to betray
her loyalty is never estranged
To God I give thee thanks
she's the answer to all the days
I preyed ..... and prayed

(Slowmotion)
Why do I feel this way?
We fit like a glove,
Now we both know this is love
The strongest kind
Us two combined
The world notices us
this is True love....
definitely necessary to discuss
indefinitely...

(CoolGmack)
It was February, when we first hooked up
Yes.. you have that good good love
I remembered..............................
you were so tight it fitted like a glove
or a hat....
Loving you was right it was bliss when we touched
in fact, this is much different from lust...
We never wanted to sever
we wanted never to give up
that's when I knew that night
you were sent from...the heavens up above

(Slowmotion)
She is that piece of mind
her piece is mine
Her and I ideas combined
Now the question is...
if it isn't love...then why do we feel this way
There is we that understand... this is crazy
Tame but torn
We are reborn
Love the rebirth
Having no doubts
on why we were....
was put here on this Earth
Love is Everything
So together this song We Sing
Our relationship

Our hop to our hip
We are the new edition
Stop.....look and listen

Shudder

Shudder to think

My mind blinks

Underestimated

Eyes dilated

In some type of rank

Shudder to think

Talked down to

Question

Who's that sound to

Loud voices

Over my choices

Shudder to think

Screaming your boat is going to sink

No words that are encouraging

Changes

They are urging

Be this

be that

Go forward

Now come back

Grow

Stifle

Be quiet because I know you have a mindful

Trying to find the missing link

Shudder to think

That I would be smarter than I look

Realizing that maturity would take as long as it took

Foreplay

Foreplay in disarray

Do not disturb on the door

Do she want more

Questioning every move

It's that time to improve

Top to bottom

She got some problems

She knows I can solve them

I'm an overachiever

I got the lick to relieve her

Turn that pain into pleasure

Focused on my mission

Put her in that position

Upfront and forward

I have this plan

I put it in her hand

Now I'll let her hold it

Take control of it

She will not misuse it

I know she don't want to lose it

Bumping that bed

My mind has been read

She does things that I only had in my imagination

And her I love tasting

We write novels on the Kamasutra and I suit her

Writing love songs

Right here is where she belongs

She does everything to please me

at the same damn time she teases me

Wetter I got to get her

cuz she does it better

Then ever

I love that touch when she bust

But this might be too much

So, let me hush

Slow and tender

No need to rush

Poets appreciation

Propped up on patience

standing on the stoops of the studious

screaming Nikki Giovanni

save me.

Let me use the great gifts

God has gave me.

The Scholars has me by the collar. Gwendolyn Brooks

I wish I could pick up the phone and call her.

Achieving incredible paragraphs

Paving those precious paths

For passionate poets

Words that I never lost

Having a Greater understanding for Robert Frost.

Saul Williams is constantly

repeating in my ears.

As I slowly climb up those stairs.

Metaphors and open doors.

Going to Florida to find Eatonville

To get that Zora Neale Hurston feel.

Writing and rhyming

Bright and blinding

Climbing that mental fence

Making it all make sense

Loving that art

Doing my part.

This is why I do this

"Success is counted sweetest"

Emily Dickinson quoting!

Shouting it out like as if it's the worlds slogan.

Properly placing the paper.

With my pen words take flight.

Beautifully bashful

But I love to write.

Sonia Sanchez echoes in the background with her stuttering sound.

Baffling and bothering.

Giant footsteps to follow in.

Writing really slow with a mellow flow.

Trying to learn to recite my poems like Maya Angelou.

"Phenomenal phenomenally" that's me.

Somehow still keeping my originality.

Past poets I give great appreciation to.

And how they just knew what they knew.

To fill Langston Hughes nice shoes. That amazing vocabulary he used.

Those incredible women and

men and where they have been.

Phrases and philosophies,

philosophies and phrases amazes.

Sets Hearts free,

Argue or agree.

For me

it's all about the poetry!

Biological

You are to psychological

I understand everything that bothers you

It's your biological

it's you being

it's your perception

you being and him fleeing

but see he had to leave to achieve what he had to achieve

there is no way you can fit your feet in his shoes

you need to understand that it was him who had more to
lose

the choice that he made wasn't his to choose

it's not anything simple to comprehend

it is his right to defend

you sit there and over-think every decision

underestimating everyone else's vision

beautiful lies there

those burdens are too heavy for one person to Bare

analyzing movements

sabotaging improvements

not wanting to be stuck in a depression state

somehow you feel as if it's not up for debate

it becomes your comfort zone

no, one wants to relate

you just feel all alone

as ears are there to listen

Arm's Reach Out To Hold

just so those burdens you can unload

wanting badly

to free all your pain understanding

The Words stability and maintain

Not wanting thoughts to run rapid in your brain.

So, you pray not to remain the same

The question is does he take all the blame

Wild Woman

Wild woman

child-like woman

free, easy and crazy

not lazy

love on her lips

in all the right places

curves and dips

exploring nothing boring

grooving and moving

life improving

slow pace to a happier place

a pleasing face

never can she forget her tears

making big steps and overcoming her fears

the woman was wild like a child excited
about learning what's new

a better future she is ready to pursue

Beautiful

Brown Beauty

I hope you see me

Be that aggressive one

My heart is undone

I become

so bashful

No hassle

Shy

I do not know how to reply

At first glance

Extremely curious to see if I have a chance

New moves to make

A big risk to take

I want you to approach me

Recognize my ability

Cherish what I have deep inside of me

Yes, brown beauty

Bursting with brilliance

This could get truly intense

I see Love In Your Eyes

You are Beyond wise

Feeling the benefits

Of the embrace

When we are placed

Face to face

We are meant

I'm daydreaming

Time well spent

I've been seeking a partnership parallel to my idea of perfe
ction

And you brown Beauty are looking right in my Direction

Luscious lyricist

can you feel this

My words are lost on your tongue

Please Release them

So, love can be what it's meant to be

That's us

You and me

Simply

However complicated

Let's relate on the educated

Nobly knowledgeable

I honor you

Full respect

On your intellect

Understand my concept

Beautiful brown Being

Your lips look relieving

No more pain once mine meets yours

Wait.............................Pause

I may be taking it to far

I see you know who you are

In a world that's so bizarre

The fragrance of your confidence

Encourages the fondness

Of my heart

Now can we start

You are

You're like an addiction

I'm not kicking

I'm with that high

When you do reply

To the important things around us

Meditation we discuss

Taking us to a place of peace

Forgetting about the hateful things ,

letting love increase

We speak on growth and the universe

Converse

Facts and perception

Education injection

Inserting knowledge so clearly

Understood

Could you hear me

Emotions

Why do you tease me?

We spoke

Emotions

Provoked

Bright windows to soul

The heart tells a story

that's never been told

Forward Fast

stronger than the past

Talking about the touch

I need you so much

Influenced by your vibe

Feeling well described

Your scent

Love letters so I can vent

Feed me Don't tease me

About the Author

Rasheeda Wiltshire aka Slowmotion was born in Port Chester Hospital raised in New Rochelle, New York. graduated New Rochelle High School.

Rasheeda always love to perform in front of an audience even though she is shy.

SlowMotion is extremely passionate about poetry. She loves open mics and respect everyone that has the courage to stand up in front of an audience and get on a mic to express themselves.

She was raised in a household full of talented women. A little fun fact, her oldest aunt on her mother's side Mary Chambers used to wake young Rasheeda up out of her sleep to perform Diana Ross for her friends. Joyce Chambers Rasheeda's youngest aunt was an amazing singer.
Aunt Brenda, Uncle James and Uncle Lou also could sing. Rasheeda's mother Virginia Chambers is the one that she h as the passion
for art. Freddy Wiltshire Rasheeda's father is where she get s the passion for rhyming. Rasheeda grew up surrounded b y a lot of love. Her grandmother Mozella Chambers Showed all her children how to Value one another. This book is dedicated to my family, Some have now gone to heaven. My mother, my father, my grandmother , both my aunts and both of my uncles. Thank God that Aunt Josette and Aunt Sue are still

living. Please show those that you hold dear to you how much you appreciate them why they're still here.

Made in the USA
Columbia, SC
09 May 2021